Stefan Herzl • Bernhard He

YOUR  KEEPSAKE

Colorama

"Beam me up, Maria"

First of all, we would like to congratulate you on acquiring this Sound of Music brochure. This little book answers questions like: Where were scenes from the film shot? Is there something besides Sound of Music in Salzburg? Whatever happened to Julie Andrews?

Stefan Herzl and I have collected a lot of material over the years and we strongly believe that we have put together the ultimate Sound of Music memory of Salzburg with this booklet.

For a Salzburg local—like myself—this Sound of Music cult has become somewhat exaggerated. My friend Julie Anne Thorpe, from Adelaide, South Australia, is a good example. When I first saw her running up and down our fields singing "The Hills are Alive", I figured that she must have a screw loose.

Actually, she inherited the Sound of Music genes from her parents. They wanted her to find and marry a guy whose last name was "Drews" so that everybody would then call her: "Julie Anne Drews". The perfect name for a real Sound of Music fan.

Call her crazy, childish, okay, but, then again, the average Sound of Music groupie is romantic and funny; and, there is really nothing wrong with that.

Cult films tend to affect people strangely. Look at the Star Trek followers: Aren't they even more nuts? They believe in beaming! Moreover, the clothes they wear are not really of the latest cut, whereas a good old Salzburg "Lederhosen" will always be in fashion.

The Sound of Music is a timeless movie and—besides being humorous and exciting—sends a message of hope, patriotism, and family strength. The songs became classics and the historical background of the von Trapp story is something that I find interesting. So, dive into the Sound of Music spirit, here in Salzburg, where both fiction and reality took place. May this little book be a helpful guide and beloved keepsake.

To the left: World famous "Getreide-gasse"–one of the narrow streets and alleys of the old town of Salzburg.

Maria and Johannes—two of the six Trapp children still alive—with co-author Bernhard Helminger (left).

Complimentary Polaroids (imprint)

Reinhard Tripp (cover illustration) is almost a Trapp but unfortunatley just a Tripp.

Stefan Herzl (writer, master-mind) told me that he never smiles in photos. A dozen polaroids later, I finally believed him. 25 years ago he had a great idea: Publishing a book about Salzburg and its Sound of Music story.

Melanie Serpa (proof reading no. 1) lives in a little gingerbread house in the country. Thank you for working long hours to help us get rid of those bloody mistakes!

Oskar Anrather (photographer) is a living legend—that's all there is to say!

Sylvia Herites (final proof reading) is a licensed Salzburg tour guide. To book her please call 0662—835151

Bernhard Helminger (graphic designer, co-author, publisher): I think this picture makes me a lot older then I actually am.

Art and Photo Credits:

Anrather: Cover, 1, 6/7, 10 (bottom), 11 (all), 12 (bottom), 46, 47 (top), 50 (both), 50 (bottom), 52 (top), 54 (left and second from top), 55 (left), 56, 57 (bottom), 62 (top); **Photo Fest:** Cover, 1, 29, 30, 31, 32, 34, 38, 39, 40, 41, 42, 47 (right), 49 (top), 57 (bottom); **Caputo:** 2, 3, 12 (second and third from top), 47 (all but top and left), 45 (bottom), 51, 53 (both), 54 (third from top), 55 (top and right), 57 (bottom); **Carolino Augusteum:** 8 (both), 9 (both); **Intern. Stiftung Mozarteum:** 10 (top); **Salzburger Festspiele:** 12 (top); **Von Trapp family:** 13 (all), 14 (all), 15 (all), 16 (both), 17, 18 (all), 19 (all), 20, 22, 24; **Salzburger Nachrichten, Vuray:** 21; **Salzburger Landespressebüro:** 23 (top); **Herzl:** 23 (bottom), 43 (both), 44 (all); **Verlag Milchstraße:** 25 (all); **Rodgers&Hammerstein Organization:** 26 (all), 27, 28 (bottom); **Martin Beck Theatre:** 28 (top); **Wild:** 35; **Helminger:** 46 (top), 53, 54 (top), 62 (second from top), 63 (right); **Verlag Böhlau:** 54 (bottom right); **Verlag St. Peter:** 48 (bottom), 52 (bottom), 63 (top); **Roubtsov:** 48, 57 (top); **Salzburger Burgen und Schlösser:** 60 (top); **Wolfgang Weinhäupl:** 62 (second from top); **Beckel:** 61, 63 (bottom left); **Salzburg Panorama Tours:** 64 (all);

Printed at Colordruck Salzburg, Vogelweiderstrasse 116, A-5020 Salzburg
Published by Colorama, Vogelweiderstrasse 116, A-5020 Salzburg (www.colorama.at)
Fourth Edition 2008, First Edition 2001 by © Colorama, All Rights Reserved
ISBN: 3-901988-00-9

Contents

Salzburg—The Sound Of Music City

Salzburg, capital of the Austrian province of the same name, has about 150,000 inhabitants. One out of three jobs is dependent directly or indirectly on tourism, but Salzburg is also a center for trading and new technologies. The university was founded by Paris Graf Lodron in 1623 and is attended by 12,000 students today.

The Founding of Salzburg

In the year 696, Bishop Rupert ("of glorious renown") was sent here from Worms on the Rhine by Duke Theodo as a missionary. He founded the Monastery of St. Peter and the Bendictine Abbey on the Nonnberg, where he installed his niece as Abbess. The actual name Salzburg was first recorded in 755 in the "Life of St. Boniface". In 774, the first cathedral was consecrated.

Salzburg became an archbishopric in the 10th century and, thanks to a clever policy of land acquisition, grew progressively. In 1077, Archbishop Gebhardt ordered the Fortresses of Hohensalzburg and Werfen to be built after he got involved in the Investiture Conflict between the pope and the German emperor. The second cathedral was built in 1300 to replace the first. The late Romanesque building can be spotted in the oldest depiction of Salzburg which dates from 1463 (see top right).

Leonhard von Keutschach became archbishop in 1495. Under his rule, the Hohensalzburg Fortress was enlarged many times and came close to how it stands today. Another important ruler was Wolf Dietrich von Raittenau who became archbishop in 1587 at the age of 28. He had the old Romanesque cathedral as well as many burgher houses pulled down to make room for the large squares that today give Salzburg its Italian style. He also erected the Residence.

Two pen-drawings (top from 1463, bottom from 1553) depicting the enormous structural progress which the fortress made under Leonhard von Keutschach.

A man just as important as the archbishop of the day was Italian architect Santino Solari. Under Archbishop Markus Sittikus, he erected today's cathedral and the world famous Hellbrunn Palace with its trick water fountains. He worked in Salzburg for 34 years and is considered to be the most successful Italian architect in German speaking areas of the 17th and 18th centuries.

Paris Graf Lodron—the "Father of the Fatherland"

Santino Solari also served during the rule of Archbishop Paris Graf Lodron (1619–1654) who ordered the architect to build fortification walls and gates. Salzburg not only had a fortress in those days—it was itself a fortress! Thanks to this and to the archbishop's clever policies, Salzburg was kept out of the Thirty Years' War.

Wheras Europe was shaken by this bloody clash in the 17th century, Salzburg remained an island of peace and shelter. That is why Paris Lodron is known as the "Father of the Fatherland" today.

In the 18th century, the fortune of the principality was not always held in the best hands. Salzburg was drawn into serveral wars. Another sad chapter was the expulsion of the Protestants by Archbishop Leopold Anton Firmian—as many as 20.000 in one year. But, the 18th century was also a period which marked the rise of the city's greatest son ...

Hey, hey, folks, my name is Wolferl! I'm the city's greatest son and I was here long before Julie Andrews rocked the hills. Don't I look great in the gala outfit Empress Maria Theresia gave me, eh?

I was born in 1756, in house number 9 on the Getreidegasse, right in the city center. At the age of four, I started to play the piano. This music stuff kind of like thrilled me and soon I composed my own musical pieces. My father Leopold became my sponsor and we traveled a lot. I met heaps of funny people: Aged 7, I was at the New Years Day Party of Louis XV from France. I performed for King George of Britain and I saw Pope Clemens XI in Rome, who even slipped me a decoration and dubbed me "Knight of the Golden Spurs".

But, most of my time I spent composing. Today, music lovers say that I wrote great operas: "Abduction from the Seraglio", "Le Nozze di Figaro", "Don Giovanni", "Così fan tutte" and "The Magic Flute". My biggest success in the charts was the "Little Night Music"-serenade. I'm sure you know the melody from commercials.

In 1774, we moved into the "Tanz-meisterhaus" on the other side of the Salzach river. Later, I lived in Vienna and Prague. After my death in 1791, my birth town gave me a number of memorials: I like the statue on my square, and for a small entrance fee, you can visit both my birthplace and my residence.

Looking forward to seeing you there,
Wolfgang Amadeus Mozart

Salzburg becomes a federal state of Austria

For more than 1000 years Salzburg was an independent principality under the rule of prince-archbishops. The prince-archbishop held the authority of the pope north of the Alps for the "Holy Roman Empire of German Nations". He had the sovereignty to mint money, hold courts of justice, and collect taxes. The salt from the Dürrnberg—the white gold—was the source of his financial success.

However, all this changed in 1803 when Archbishop Hieronymus Graf Colloredo fled to Vienna to escape the advancing Napoleonic troops. The time for secularisation had finally come.

In 1816, Salzburg became a federal state of Austria and established a provincial government.

Salzburg landmarks: inside and outside the Salzburg Cathedral and the Hohensalzburg Fortress.

The Salzburg Festival

The Festival was founded in 1920, when director Max Reinhardt staged Hofmannsthal's "Everyman". The play has been part of the Festival program ever since and is always performed on the same spot—in front of the cathedral.

When, in 1924, Max Reinhardt succeeded with his plan to reconstruct a section of the former court stables to accommodate a provisional festival theater, nobody imagined that this temporary solution would grow into today's enormous Festival House.

Today, the Festival House accommodates three theaters: Seating 1,324 people, the Small Festival Hall is by no means small. It was only called so after the completion of the Large Hall in 1960. The Rock Riding School is certainly Salzburg's most original theater. Its 96 arcades, created in 1693, are ingeniously combined with the stage settings. The venue also features a roof that opens and closes within 40 seconds.

In all, around 5,000 people can participate in different cultural performances on one given evening.

Past and present at the Salzburg Festival (from top): The first "Everyman" in front of the cathedral in 1920 and the production from 1998; the façade of the Festival House —built under the rule of Wolf Dietrich in 1607; inside the Large Festival Hall.

Georg Ritter von Trapp

Georg Ritter von Trapp was born on April 4th, 1880, in Zara (now Zadar), Croatia, then still part of the Austrian-Hungarian Empire. His father was a navy captain. He wanted to embark on a navy career as well and attended the Royal Naval Academy in Fiume (now Rijeka).

In 1910, he met Agathe Whitehead at a ball. It was love at first sight and their marriage a society event. While still a young navy captain, the command of the submarine "U6" was assigned to him. During World War One, the French submarine "Leon Gambetta" was sunk by

Picture above: Captain von Trapp as a highly decorated navy commander.

Pictures below (from left to right): Captain von Trapp (seated) on submarine "U5"; submarine "U14" was captured from the French in 1914 and later commanded by Captain Trapp; an exact diary had to be kept in wartimes—Captain Trapp dictates to his secretary.

Trapp's mission. In 1918, he was promoted to lieutenant commander by Emperor Franz Josef I.

After the war, Austria lost its access to the coast and did not need a navy. Captain von Trapp not only lost his post, but also his wife. Lady Whitehead died in 1924 and left him alone with seven children to look after. In 1938, Austria was annexed to Adolf Hitler's German Empire and Captain von Trapp was offered a high position in its navy. "I have sworn my oath of loyality to only one Emperor" was his answer—he rejected.

Pictures (from above): Captain von Trapp; Captain von Trapp and Lady Whitehead at their wedding in 1910; the couple with five of their seven children.

Maria Augusta von Kutschera

Maria Augusta von Kutschera was born on a train on its way to Vienna on January 25th, 1905. Her mother died when she was about two years old and Maria grew up with a foster mother (an elderly cousin of her fathers) in a little house on the outskirts of Vienna. She underwent a very strict education without any other children around. She spent five years in a grade school followed by three years in a high school and four years in a State Teachers College.

Pictures (clockwise): Maria's first-communion photo; Maria in authentic Austrian costume; the wedding at the Nonnberg Abbey; the Trapp villa in Salzburg.

Raised as a socialist and atheist, her attitude changed dramatically when, intending to hear a Bach concert, she entered her college church. A well known priest, Father Kronseder, started to preach and Maria found herself overwhelmed by what he had to say. A meeting with this priest changed Maria's life and belief.

Maria joined the Nonnberg Abbey in Salzburg to become a nun. It was decided that Maria should leave the convent for a year to go to the Trapp Villa to work as a governess for the baron's daughter who lay in bed with rheumatic fever.

Above: Maria von Trapp at the Vermont chalet in the early 70's
Left: Maria and her husband—Captain von Trapp.

After the first year, the children asked their father to do something to make their governess stay. They even suggested he should marry her. "I don't even know if she likes me!", was the baron's answer. So, the children went to ask for themselves. As Maria said "Yes, I do", they were engaged. She never returned to the abbey, and married the Baron on November 26th, 1927.

The Trapp Family

Two more daughters were born and the von Trapps were content. In 1935, Father Wasner entered their lives. It was he who brought sophistication to the family hobby—music. The natural freshness and purity of their voices awarded them the first prize in a choral competition during the Salzburg Festival in 1935. The family, who had lost all its money during the depression, was invited to give concerts throughout Europe.

In 1938, Hitler entered Austria and the von Trapps decided to save their spiritual rather than their material wealth and left their large estate outside of Salzburg for the United States.

As if going out for one of their usual family hikes with knapsacks on their backs and dressed in mountaineering clothes, they left their house and belongings behind. They took trains through the Austrian Alps, crossing the border to Italy and on through Switzerland, then France to London, and finally a boat to America.

Below: One of the last pictures taken of the Trapp family in Salzburg before Hitler took over Austria on March 11th, 1938. The Hohensalzburg Fortress can be seen in the photo's background.

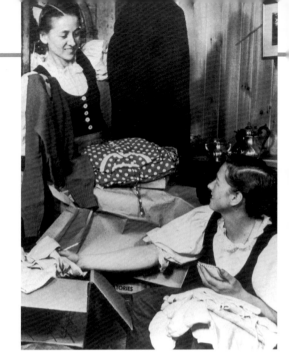

In September 1938, they arrived in New York. There were nine children with a tenth on the way, and they were accompanied by Father Wasner, who had become their family chaplain. Under his direction, singing turned into a profession and they became known as "The Trapp Family Singers". The family traveled throughout the United States for eight months on concert tours. After this period, their US-visa expired and the Family

Singers were forced to leave the country. Thanks to concert invitations, however, they managed to get visas for Scandinavian countries.

When World War II broke out in September 1939, their American manager sent them tickets for the next crossing, so that they could fulfill their contracts with him.

After World War II, the Trapp Family started a musical charity organisation: "Trapp Family Austrian Relief Inc.". The family sent countless parcels of food and clothing back to their homeland Austria.

Photo to the left: The bus with "The Trapp Family Singers" painted on it was their only home during their first two years in the United States.

Starting a Life in Vermont

In 1941, the Trapp family bought a large farm in Vermont, in a countryside very similar to the Austrian landscape near Salzburg that they missed. The house they lived in was called "Cor Unum", which means "one heart".

Trapp family members building their new home in Stowe, Vermont.

On May 30th, 1947, Georg Ritter von Trapp passed away in Stowe. He is buried in the family cemetery in a meadow behind the lodge.

When their singing career came to an end, after nearly twenty years of concerts in over thirty countries, they turned their big Austrian chalet into a lodge. In December 1980, their lodge burned to the ground. The future loomed before them— and they immediately planned to rebuild. The new Trapp Family Lodge is built for the future with the flavor of the past.

A logical outgrowth of the Lodge and its rebuilding has been the Family Guest House program. Offered on a timeshare basis, the guest houses have helped the Trapp family to avoid disappointing the many people who are unable to get reservations in the limited number of lodge rooms. Guest house ownership assures accomodations at your favorite place when you want it.

On March 28th, 1987, Maria Augusta passed away in Stowe. She rests next to her husband in the family cemetery.

In 1940, the career of the Trapp Family Singers was advanced by their new agent – Freddy Schang from Columbia Concerts. Their fee rose to $1,000 per concert, the annual tours expanded from 60 to finally 125, and they were dubbed "the most heavily booked attraction in concert history". And, yes, in 1952, the Trapp Singers even made it to Hawaii (picture below).

Prelate Franz Wasner

Prelate Franz Wasner was born on December 28th, 1905, in Feldkirchen, a small farming community in Upper Austria. After completing his studies in theology at the University of Innsbruck, he was ordained a priest on March 17th, 1929, and served in the small parish of Mayrhofen in Tyrol for one year. Then he went to Rome to study ecclesiastical law and graduated summa cum laudae as "Dr jur can" in 1934.

Wasner returned to Salzburg where he met Georg von Trapp. This acquaintance grew into a close friendship and Father Wasner accompanied the Trapp family as director and conductor on all their concert tours.

During a tour in Australia and New Zealand, he decided to do missionary work on the Fiji Islands until 1966. He returned again to Salzburg, but only for a short time. The Vatican called on him to become the rector of the "Anima", the home of German-speaking theology students in Rome, which enjoyed great influx under Prelate Wasner's leadership of more than 15 years.

Prelate Wasner received many honors from several countries as recognition for his devoted service. He passed away in June 1992 in Salzburg.

Father Wasner attending mass back home in Salzburg.

The Trapp Family Today

Rupert (born in 1911) practiced as a medical doctor until the mid-80's and died at the age of 80. He had six children.

Agathe (born in 1913) lives near Baltimore, Maryland and used to work for a kindergarten. She still returns to Salzburg from time to time.

After 27 years of missionary work in New Guinea, **Maria** (born in 1914) now lives in Stowe, Vermont.

Werner (born in 1915) became a farmer and had six children. He passed away on October 11th, 2007.

Hedwig (born in 1917) worked at the lodge until her death in 1972.

Johanna (born in 1919) married in 1948 and left America to return to her homeland Austria. She lived in Vienna until her death in 1994 and had six children.

Martina (born in 1921) stayed with her family until she married in 1949. She died in childbirth in 1951.

Rosemarie (born in 1929) lives in Stowe, Vermont.

Eleonore (born in 1931) stopped singing in 1952, got married in 1954 and raised seven children.

Johannes Georg (born in 1939) graduated from Dartmouth, has a Master's Degree in forestry (Yale) and is now president of the Trapp Family Lodge. He has two children.

In 1998, on the occasion of the Broadway Revival of The Sound of Music, Arno Gasteiger, vice governor of Salzburg, presented the remaining six von Trapp children with the state's highest civilian decoration, the Golden Decoration of Honour, in New York. Gasteiger also presented medals to seven actors who portrayed the von Trapp family children in the movie. Above: The Trapp family with Arno Gasteiger, New York, 1998.

Pictures below: Maria von Trapp (daughter)

The story of the Trapp family has not only been a story of triumph but loss. In December 1980, a couple of days before Christmas, their Vermont inn burned down to the ground. The rebuilding process was a lengthy one. In 1983, the new Trapp Family Lodge opened its doors to the first visitors.

Picture: The new Trapp Family Lodge at Christmastime.

The Book

It all started when Maria von Trapp decided to write a book about the adventurous life of the Trapp family. "The Story of the Trapp Family" was published in 1949 and it was not long before Hollywood wanted to buy the book title. As they only wanted to use the title without the story, however, Maria refused.

The German Films

Some years later, in 1956, Wolfgang Reinhardt (son of the famous stage director Max Reinhardt) made an offer of $ 10,000. By signing his offer, Maria unwillingly gave away all film rights (and the right to royalties). Not only did he make her believe she could not get any royalties from the German film—as she had meanwhile become a US citizen—but he even phoned a few weeks later asking her to accept $ 9,000 in cash at once. Maria needed the money and accepted.

"Die Trapp Familie" and it's sequel "Die Trapp Familie in Amerika" became a big success in Germany and later in Europe and South America.

Pictures to the left: Ruth Leuwerik (as "Maria") and Hans Holt (as "Captain") starred in "Die Trapp Familie"—the German version of the von Trapp story.

The Broadway Play

It was Paramount Pictures that bought the film rights the same year (1956). After viewing the German film, Vincent Donahue, Broadway and television director, saw a perfect role for Mary Martin, a Broadway star he had worked with earlier ("Annie get your gun").

Maria von Trapp (center) greets two of her stage alter-egos: On the right, Florence Henderson, star of the first U.S. National Tour, and on the left Mary Martin, star of the original Broadway production.

(Picture courtesy of The Rodgers&Hammerstein Organization)

(Pictures courtesy of The Rodgers&Hammerstein Organization)

Mary Martin as "Maria" and Theodore Bikel as "Captain von Trapp" starred in the original Broadway production of The Sound Of Music, which opened on November 16th, 1959, and ran for three years.

In the meantime Paramount had dropped the option and no longer owned the film rights, so Donahue contacted Maria in New Guinea, where she was doing missionary work. She did not answer his letters because she was not at all interested in her book being performed on Broadway. But Richard Halliday, Mary Martin's husband and producer, did not give up and finally persuaded Maria to see his wife in "Annie Get Your Gun". Maria was impressed and reversed her opinion. Halliday made a deal with the German producers and shared the royalties with Maria.

Rodgers and Hammerstein wrote the music and acted as coproducers. The show had 1,443 performances, won six Tony Awards (one for Best Musical) and sold over 3 million albums. It was the filming of the story, however, that made The Sound of Music world famous, and so popular that today nearly every English speaking child is raised with its songs.

Picture below: Mary Martin joined by the songwriters, composer Richard Rodgers (left) and Lyricist Oscar Hammerstein II (right).

(Picture courtesy of The Rodgers&Hammerstein Organization)

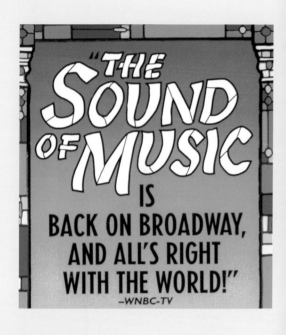

Poster to the right: 1998 was the year of a big Sound of Music Broadway Revival. Again, the Sound of Music magic worked; it had not faded in all these years.

Rebecca Luker and Michael Siberry played the "von Trapps" and Susan H. Schulman directed at New York's Martin Beck Theatre.

(Picture courtesy of The Rodgers&Hammerstein Organization)

The writers of The Sound of Music (1959) from left to right: composer Richard Rodgers, lyricist Oscar Hammerstein II, and scriptwriters Howard Lindsay and Russel Crouse.

The Sound of Music film

On the opening night of the musical there were many famous people in the audience, but for the eventual filming of The Sound of Music just two of the people in the crowd were important: Irving "Swifty" Lazar, who represented the show's writers and Spyros Skouras, president of Twentieth Century Fox.

Skouras loved the play and a few months later he bought the rights for the film for 1.25 million dollars. The contract stated that he was not to release the film until 1964 or after the closing of the show. It was The Sound of Music project that helped Century Fox in a time of increasing financial difficulties. After some trouble finding the right director, Ernest Lehmann (who had already scripted "The King and I" and "The West Side Story") and studio chief Richard Zanuck won over their first choice, Robert Wise, as director of the movie.

From the film: The von Trapps singing "Edelweiss" at the Rock Riding School.

Julie Andrews

Julie Andrews was the only one director Robert Wise considered seriously for the role of "Maria".

The actress, born in Walton-on-Thames, England on October 1st, 1935, was a former child star of British revues and a very successful Broadway star ("The Boy Friend", "My Fair Lady", "Camelot"). Her theatrical training made her ideally suited to the filmmaking style that had had its heyday in the Hollywood musicals of the 1940's and 1950's.

Her cinematic persona was established with her first appearence on screen as the magical title character in Walt Disney's "Mary Poppins" (one of the top grossing films of all times). Winning an Oscar for "Mary Poppins" was also a personal coup for Andrews. Just before getting the role, she had lost the role of Eliza Doolittle ("My Fair Lady") to Audrey Hepburn.

Andrew's portrayals of Mary Poppins and Maria von Trapp not only placed her at the forefront of bankable Hollywood stars of the 60's, but marked and, in effect, pigeonholed her career. She created strict but loving figures whose no-nonsense manner hid magical powers.

After a while, Julie Andrews became tired of her squeaky clean screen portrayals and like most actors, sought different kinds of roles. Thanks to her films with husband Blake Edwards she has succeeded in changing the sugar image that has followed her throughout her career.

In 1982, she earned another Academy Award nomination for "Victor/Victoria" which suggested that she had, at last, broken free of her "singing governess" image and had embarked on a promising new phase in her career.

Julie Andrews has lived in Los Angeles since the early 1990's with her husband and five children, two of whom are adopted from Vietnam. After an unsuccessful operation in 1997, she lost her voice entirely for one year. As a result of that, she began writing children's books ("Mandy" was published in October 1999). On 31st of December 1999, Queen Elizabeth II knighted Julie Andrews as a Dame. The actress celebrated an incredible film comeback with "The Princess Diaries" (Parts I and II in 2001 and 2004 respectively) and as the voice of Princess Fiona's mother in "Shrek 2" (2004).

Other Films:

1966	Torn Curtain, Hawaii
1967	Thoroughly Modern Millie, The Singing Princes (animation)
1968	Star! (director Robert Wise)
1970	Darling Lili
1974	The Tamarind Sea
1979	10
1980	Little Miss Baker
1981	S.O.B.
1982	Victor/Victoria
1983	The Man Who Loved A Woman
1984	Hanya: Portrait of a Dance Legend
1985	Pandora's Box
1986	Duet for One, That's Life!
1991	Cin Cin, Our Sons
2000	Relative values

Christopher Plummer

Before The Sound of Music, he was a famous Shakespearean actor, having played only once in a major film—"The Fall of the Roman Empire".

Plummer didn't like The Sound of Music, or the children. For years he called it "The Sound of Mucus". The children didn't have to act as if they were afraid of him—they really were! When he had to carry "Gretl" over the mountains in the escape scene, he said: "I'm not carrying that bloody fat kid", so Robert Wise got a thinner child as her double.

He only did the film because he wanted to sing and then got dubbed in the last minute; his voice wasn't full enough next to Julie Andrews'.

However, he suited the role of a noble widower perfectly. After his success with The Sound of Music, he appeared in numerous movies and still works in film, television and stage today.

Eleanor Parker

A movie actress at the age of 18, Eleanor Parker became famous in the 50's with three Academy Award nominations for

The ballroom scene: Captain von Trapp (Christopher Plummer, center), the Baroness (Eleonor Parker, right) and Maria (Julie Andrews, left).

Peggy Wood as Mother Abbess (left).

"Caged", "Detective Story" and "Interrupted Melody". She was the "name" Wise counted on, as she had been known for many years. After The Sound of Music, Parker retired to Palm Springs.

Richard Haydn (Max Detweiler)

Originally, Haydn was a dancer, but became active in movies after working with a itinerate film company in Jamaica, where he was living at the time. Wise chose him for his comedian talent and engaging personality. He died on April 25th, 1985.

Peggy Wood (Mother Abbess)

Peggy Wood was a grande dame of the American Theater, not often seen on the movie screen. The Sound of Music took her back to her roots, as she had started her career as a musical actress. Wood liked her part as the warmhearted Mother Abbess although her voice had to be dubbed. She died on March 18th, 1978.

The Children

Charmian Carr (Liesl)

Not intending to be an actress, she worked part-time as a model. A friend of Carr's sent a picture of her to director Robert Wise. He discovered that she was able to dance and sing and—there she was—a perfect "Liesl".

At 21 no longer a child, she was included in the nightly parties at which Christopher Plummer played the piano and sang.

Her most memorable scene was dancing in the gazebo while singing "Sixteen Going On Seventeen": Wearing new shoes, she gracefully jumped to the bench and flew on through a plate-glass window spraining her ankle. She was bandaged up, swallowed two aspirins and went on to dance. The crew gave her standing ovations at the end of the day which proved to be one of the most fulfilling of her life.

Today, a grandmother, she runs an interior design business in California with a list of famous clients like Michael Jackson.

Nicholas Hammond (Friedrich)

Nobody thought he would get the role —he couldn't sing at the audition, after he had lost his front teeth in a ski accident a few days before. Maybe he was cast because he was already a professional with television, Broadway and movie appearances.

Hammond loved playing Friedrich but the role had its difficult moments: On the night before filming started, Robert Wise surprised the crew with a direct order: "I want him blond in the morning!" The transformation of his hair color from chestnut to blond took more than a day, so, in the scenes which were shot first, one notices that Friedrichs hair appears darker then otherwise (e. g. thunderstorm scene: "My favorite things"). The hair dyeing—executed by Marilyn Monroe's hairdresser—also left the thirteen-year-old with blisters which took weeks to heal.

Later, Hammond was "Spiderman" in the TV series. He now works as a scriptwriter in Sydney, Australia.

Angela Cartwright (Brigitta)

The eleven-year-old was already known for her role in the sequel "Make room for Daddy" when she was cast for The Sound of Music. After the film she starred in the series "Lost in Space" and made her living as a film actress. Presently, she lives in Los Angeles with her husband and her two children and runs an Internet gift shop.

Heather Menzies (Louisa)

She got the role although she lacked experience. After the film, she starred in television series and other movies. She has

In the year 2000, thirty-six years after The Sound of Music hit the big screen, a TV documentary reunited the children in Salzburg. From left: Carr, Turner, Chase, Cartwright, Menzies, Karath and Hammond.

been married to actor Robert Urich for 25 years and lives in California. They have three children. Heather was 14 when she played "Louisa".

Duane Chase (Kurt)

He started his career at the age of eleven doing commercials and was thirteen when he played "Kurt". Today, he works as a computer software designer in Seattle.

Debbie Turner (Marta)

Turner too started in commercials and was seven when she played "Marta". Today, she is married to an aircraft technician. They have four daughters. She lives in Minnesota and runs a business making Santa Claus figures.

Kym Karath (Gretl)

She had already done three movies before The Sound of Music. Robert Wise knew instantly he would never find another 5-year–old with such camera presence. She doesn't remember much of the filming, but of course it was impossible for her to keep up with the older children, especially in regards to the boat scene. Not being able to swim, she "drank half the lake". To this day, she is afraid of water.

Karath starred in "All my children" before taking time off for her son who was born in 1991. She lives in Greenwich, Connecticut, and is married to an investment banker.

The Plot

Maria, a novice in a strict Salzburg Abbey, loves the majestic landscape of the Alps and often forgets about religious duties hiking on "her" hills. Mother Abbess, a very wise woman, thinks Maria might be better suited for life outside the convent and decides to sends her to Baron von Trapp's villa to act as a governess for his seven children.

Upon arriving at the villa, Maria is surprised at the military discipline in which the children are subjected by their father, a noble and widowed naval officer. She discovers she is the latest of many governesses that the children have already driven away. Maria takes a different approach to the children. Instead of educating them, she introduces music to their lives, teaching them how to sing and play and laugh—and so, is rewarded with the children's love.

A puppet show, staged by the children for their father, is the first step towards a blooming love between Maria and the baron. Only a few days later, however, the Baron presents Baroness Schroeder as his fiancée to his children. During a ball, the baron and Maria stage a folklore dance for the audience and—while dancing with each other—discover their feelings. Baroness Schroeder encourages Maria to leave the Trapp Villa at once. She flees to the convent.

The children soon feel Maria's loss and think about ways to make her come back, while the baron decides to marry Baroness Schroeder. Maria, back in the convent, confesses her love for the baron and wise Mother Abbess makes her "Climb evr'y mountain" for her love. She hurries back to the Trapp Villa only to find the baron set on the marriage. The baroness, however, recognises the true love between the baron and Maria and leaves. Accompanied by seven children, Maria marries the man she loves in the Abbey where she had wanted to become a nun.

Fate strikes. When they return from their honeymoon, the Nazis have already occupied Austria. The baron plans to escape from forced naval service and sees his opportunity: The whole family takes part in a chorus festival at the Salzburg Festival Hall. Here is where the baron sings his "Edelweiss", a dedication to his beloved country—hours before leaving it forever. The von Trapps make a dramatic escape after hiding in the Abbey cemetery.

The final scene sees the Trapp family climbing the Alps to safely reach Switzerland —the dawn symbolizing their new life ahead.

The Director—Robert Wise

Through his wide range of work, Robert Wise proved himself to be a highly versatile director. How else can it be explained that the same director staged horror classics like "The Haunting" and "The Body Snatcher" as well as family movies like "The Sound of Music" or "West Side Story". For the former two, Robert Wise received Oscars for Best Director.

The son of a meat packer—born in Winchester, Indiana, on September 19th, 1914—Wise studied journalism at the Franklin College, but due to financial problems he had to leave school and find work. Aged 19, he was hired as assistant editor at Hollywood's RKO studios, where his brother David was employed.

His first directorial opportunity just fell into his lap: Director Gunther von Fritsch, who was already half way through with "The Curse of the Cat People", was dismissed because he was behind schedule. Robert Wise was the editor of the movie, and it was natural for him to take over and complete the film, since only he knew the continuity of what had already been shot. He did such an admirable job that his boss Val Lewton assigned him as full director.

His cinematography continued with such films as "The Day the Earth Stood Still", "Somebody Up There Likes Me" (with Paul Newman) and "Run Silent, Run Deep" (Burt Lancaster, Clark Gable).

Robert Wise passed away on September 14th, 2005, just days after celebrating his 91st birthday.

Robert Wise (to the left) on set.

A Film is Made

Salzburg is more than just a city where this story took place. It is an atmosphere— Robert Wise

Location scouting in Salzburg began in 1963 and filming on location started in early spring of 1964. Robert Wise had planned to spend six weeks shooting on location as the flights and the housing for over 250 crew members, technicians, camera men, stage hands, architects and actors were extremely expensive and there were even more technicians coming from Munich, Germany. The schedules were quite tight. The only thing that could not be planned was weather, and as Salzburg is famous for its rain, the six weeks turned out to be eleven.

One day the crew was visited by an unexpected guest—Maria von Trapp herself. She was visiting Salzburg and asked to take part in the film. Wise decided to have her as an extra in the scene where Andrews walks towards the fountain on the Residence square singing "I have Confidence in Me". Baroness von Trapp experienced a three hour shooting and is reported to have said in the end "That's one ambition I'm giving up!". She and Christopher Plummer (left) became friends (center: director Robert Wise).

During location scouting the settings had been chosen: Frohnburg Castle, a 17th century castle on the outskirts of the city, for the front courtyard. Today, the castle houses students of the Mozarteum Music Academy. Leopoldskron Castle was chosen for the setting on the lake, its garden and the terrace leading down to the water. In reality, it is used for international seminars and conferences.

When the weather was bad the crew could shoot in covered sets. One was St. Magret's Chapel (e. g. for the beginning scene when the nuns pray) and the other were studios in nearby Parsch.

The company was housed in four hotels: Wise and Andrews stayed at the "Österreichischer Hof", the children at the "Parkhotel Mirabell", Plummer and the nuns at the "Bristol" and the rest of the crew at the "Winkler". The production office was in the Dürer Studios, make-up and hairdressing at the Bristol. The working schedule was six days a week.

"Do-Re-Mi"—which was rehearsed in the Fox Studios beforehand—was shot all over the city, sometimes leaving the bypassers wondering where all the loud music was coming from. One of the hard things

for Julie Andrews in this scene was that she was not capable of playing the guitar and singing at the same time. Once, when the producer got really angry, Andrews took a glass of "firewater"—pure Austrian Schnapps—and everything went well!

The central spot for the actors' off-screen scene turned out to be the bar at the Bristol. There were big crew parties almost every night. Plummer's nights at the bar became famous, but the next morning he acted with as much professionalism as usual.

Julie Andrews felt slightly isolated as she had to take care of her 18-month-old daughter in the evenings and could not go out as often as she wanted.

The children behaved very well during their strenuous film work, but loved to play tricks on people in their free time. Sometimes, when their mothers were away, they threw things from the hotel windows on unsuspecting bypassers. One of their famous jokes was taking all the shoes on the second floor—which had been put outside the hotelroom doors to be polished—and exchanging them with those from the third floor. That created quite a confusion the next morning! The hotel wanted them to leave after the shoe joke and it was Robert Wise who calmed them all down.

For the children, Salzburg was quite an adventure. During their free time, their teacher, Jean Seaman, showed them the sights and taught them German. The attraction they liked most were the trick water fountains at Hellbrunn Palace, where they laughed a lot getting wet from unexpected angles.

Kym Karath has some frightening memories of the shooting. During the canoe scene the children had to fall out of the boat. Karath could not swim. Julie Andrews was supposed to catch her, but what went well in the first take, went wrong in the second one: Julie went off the wrong side of the boat and Alan Callow had to jump in to save the little star.

During the shooting another problem arose: the children were growing, some more than the others. "Liesl", Charmian Carr, did not, so to keep up the continuity she had to stand on an apple box in the end. In her free time, she worked on a documentary of the filming of The Sound of Music which was used as a trailer in the theatres before the release of the film.

And, then there was the teeth problem! Debbie Turner lost some of her baby teeth during shooting and they had to be replaced which caused her troubles with the singing. One day, Richard Haydn dropped his dentures into the toilet without having a second pair with him.

One of the first scenes that could be shot on location was the wedding scene at Mondsee. That was on April 23rd. Nearly all exterior scenes could be shot on location, although the rain kept returning. There were just a few that could not be shot on location and these were rebuilt in the studios: "Sixteen going on Seventeen"

Strolling along the Salzach river banks

and "Something Good". The interior of the gazebo was difficult to film as sunlight came in from different angles. And, for the other effects like rain and lightning it was less expensive to film in the studios.

One of the most complicated shootings was the family's appearance in the Rock Riding School. There were a thousand extras sitting in the audience in summer clothes, though it was just a bit above zero. The lighting of the arches turned out to be difficult. Lights and generators from all over Europe had to be ordered.

The opening scene that became one of the most famous in film history was filmed on a mountain about 10 kilometers into Bavaria. The scene was shot from a helicopter and had to be perfectly timed, so one of the crew members hid in the bushes with a megaphone and yelled "Go, Julie" when the helicopter was in the right position. Julie Andrews had great difficulty standing upright because of the jet helicopter's strong downward drafts. After ten takes she got really angry! The filming up there was strenuous for the crew members. Apart from the weather playing tricks on them, there were no toilets for miles and sometimes it was just freezing.

When filming was 25 days behind schedule, the studio started to put pressure on because the budget was exploding.

On Friday, July 3rd, after having shot the last part of "The hills are Alive", Wise returned home with the crew and on July 6th, they started the indoor shooting in the studios. The movie was released on March 2nd, 1965 at the Rivoli Theatre in New York. Movie theaters throughout America were sold out for weeks: sobbing could be heard every time Christopher Plummer stood on the stage of the Festival Hall to sing "Edelweiss", "16" was a wonderful age to be; and, learning to sing was as easy as "Do Re Mi". Salzburg suddenly became the city of The Sound of Music.

From the film: "The hills Are alive"— one of the lovely scenes shot in the surrounding areas of Salzburg (left).

The Sound of Music in the 21st Century

"The Sound of Music" has lost none of its fascination almost 50 years since the stage musical premiere and 40 years since the film debut. While there is speculation about a remake of the film, a comeback of the musical in London is certain: none less than Andrew Lloyd Webber is set to bring it back to the stage again. The actress to play Maria is to be picked on a reality television show. No further information about the production schedule was at hand at the time of this book's publication.

In February 2005, Viennese opera audiences reacted with surprise when one of the city's most renowned theatres, the Volksoper, staged a production of "The Sound of Music". Nevertheless, the French-Canadian production by Renaud Doucet (Director and Choreograper) and André Barbe (Sets and Costumes) received national and international acclaim and was a hit with audiences. Erich Kunzel, leader of the Cincinnati Pops Orchestra and Grammy Award winner, could be secured for the conductor's role. Maria was played by the Austro-Australian singer, Sandra Pires. Born in East Timor, Sandra moved to Australia when she was 13. She was only 15 when she won the nation's most important singing-competition.

"The Sound of Music" at the Volksoper: The role of Baron von Trapp is performed by internationally acclaimed baritone Michael Kraus (picture below).

Over 450 children auditioned to fill the six coveted children's roles in the musical, the largest response ever received by the Volksoper for an children's casting call.

The stage version at the Volksoper is performed and sung in German with English surtitles. The next performances will be staged in October 2006, but due to the roaring success the musical will stay in the repertoire for a long time.

40th Anniversary of "The Sound of Music" as Film

2005 was the 40th anniversary of the film premiere of the "The Sound of Music", an occasion for which 20th Century Fox and the Austrian National Tourist Office hosted a big celebration in New York.

The emotional party reunited Julie Andrews with her seven "film children"— the first in twenty years! Together the

Julie Andrews re-united with her "film children": From left to right: Charmian Carr, Nicholas Hammond, Angela Cartwright, Heather Menzies, Julie Andrews, Debbie Turner, Kym Karath and Duane Chase.

actors reminisced about their experiences during the nine-week shooting of the film. At the end of the media engagement, the actors gathered around the piano with Johannes von Trapp to sing "Edelweiss".

Director Robert Wise could no longer be there, since he died of a heart attack on September 14th, four days after his 91st birthday. His widow, Pamela Wise, was among the honoured guests, however, as were Alice Hammerstein Mathias, the daughter of librettist Oscar Hammerstein II, and Mary Rodgers Guettel, daughter of the composer Richard Rogers. Enthusiastic fans gathered on New York's Time Square in front of the studio, dressed as nuns and Marias with "The Hills are Alive" ringing out over wintry Times Square.

A double-DVD was released for the 40th anniversary. Several bonus features were added along with the original film, including a 22-minute documentary tour

"On Location in Salzburg", filmed and produced by Charmian Carr. The new DVD was already a hit seller days before the official release date.

Picture above: Julie Andrews at the party in New York. Would you believe that this shining star is already in her 70's?

Picture to the left: The star of the evening with Michael Gigl, Director Austrian National Tourist Office New York and Panorama Tours CEO Stefan Herzl.

The Sound of Christmas

Julie Andrews returned to Salzburg in 1987 for the "The Sound of Christmas". This television special was designed to be a scenic and tuneful holiday with friends like Placido Domingo, John Denver and the King's Singers, a famous British choral group. The one hour show recalled scenes of the Oscar-winning movie. Christopher Plummer declined the invitation to come back to the Sound of Music locations.

Framed by the spectacular Alps, Julie Andrews sang a new yuletide number, "The Sound of Christmas". Another sequence took place at the church of Mondsee, where Julie's character, Maria, was

married in the film. The church's baroque interior reverberated with the sound of Placido's rendition of "O Holy Night" and with the caroling of the ensemble.

Many film producers have previously made use of Leopoldskron Palace due to its unique location. The "Sound of Christmas" crew decided to shoot inside the rococo building, whereas, for the original Hollywood production, only the terrace and the gardens were used.

Picture above: Julie Andrews and Placido Domingo.

Picture to the left: The couple accompanied by John Denver and other singers.

Other highlights included: a comic version of "The Twelve Days of Christmas" by Julie and the King's Singers, "Dancing with the Mountains", a showcase for John Denver on skis, an elaborate waltz medley set in the ornate Leopoldskron Palace, Julie's haunting interpretation of "In the Bleak Mid-winter", Christina Rosetti's poem set to the music by Gustav Holst taped in Hohenwerfen Fortress, and a couple of duets: "Something New in My Life" and, of course, "Edelweiss".

Pictures to the left: Julie Andrews singing in front of the Horsepond and John Denver with a drink that Salzburg is also famous for.

A high honour: On the occasion of the Christmas production, Julie Andrews and director Robert Wise were awarded the "decoration in gold" by the head of the Salzburg government, Hans Katschthaler.

Mirabell Palace and Gardens

Its characteristic, large, symmetrical flower-beds make the Mirabell Gardens a good example of a typical baroque park. It was built in the 18th century following the plans of the famous architect Fischer von Erlach. Countless statues inspired by greek myths can be seen throughout the park which is centered by a big fountain.

In the film, Maria and the children danced around the Fountain singing "Do-re-mi" *(see picture on page 34)*. The Pegasus fountain next to the 17th century palace can also be spotted in the movie. The stairs leading up to the rose hill were part of the choreography as well.

Nonnberg Abbey

Nonnberg Abbey is the oldest female convent north of the Alps. It has been in continual existence since it was founded in the year 714 A.D.

In the course of its history, the abbey was destroyed by fire several times, but it was always rebuilt by the rulers of the city and the church. Today's building was erected in the early 16th century. The wooden gothic altar by the sculptor Veit Stoss is especially worth seeing. It is located in the St. John's Chapel near the gate.

The Abbey on the Nonnberg is significant both for the real Trapp story as well as for the movie.

After graduating from college, Maria Augusta von Kutschera took a train to Salzburg to present herself as a candidate for the novitiate of the Benedictine sisterhood. After serving as a governess outside the abbey she and Baron von Trapp married in the Abbey Church in 1927.

The Sound of Music scenes shot here include the opening part where the nuns go to mass and Maria returns too late. The performance for the song "Maria" was staged in the courtyard of the abbey. The children came to the abbey's gate to ask Maria to return to their home (see picture). The escape scene, with the cars parked outside the Abbey gate, was also shot in the original spot.

Pictures on the left (from above): The tower of the abbey church; the gate where the children saw Mother Abbess; the abbey's courtyard; inside the church.

The Horse Pond next to the Festival Building is another sight a lot of people associate with The Sound of Music. It was built in 1695 by Austrian architect Fischer von Erlach. Before being part of the Sound of Music scenery, it served as a watering-place for the Archbishop's riding stables.

After the Trapp family left Austria, their beautiful villa was annexed by Himmler. It became the telephone headquarters for the Third Reich. After the war, the Trapp family sold the estate to the Roman catholic church.

Today, the villa houses a seminary for young missionaries from the order "Brothers of the Holy Blood". Visitors of the original Trapp home are allowed to go into the gardens, but are asked to keep quiet and not to enter the house.

Rock Riding School (Festival House)

For the construction of the cathedral rocks were cut out from the Mönchsberg. In 1693, Archbishop Johann Ernst von Thun decided to use this cavity in the mountain and had a riding school built in which tournaments were held. Today the Rock Riding School is a theater and one of the venues situated in the Festival District.

The "real" Trapp family sang here at a choir competition. In the motion picture, Christopher Plummer sang "Edelweiss" in the Rock Riding School while their escape was organized behind the curtain.

The Archbishop's Residence

The Residence Square is the heart of the old city center. In the film, Maria crossed this square singing "I have confidence in me" while on her way to the Trapp family home for the first time.

The Glockenspiel with its 35-bell chime overlooks the square. It was cast in 1689 in Antwerp by Melchior de Haze.

The Residence buildings were used by the prince archbishops from the 17th century onwards. Apart from being archbishops, they also held absolute power over Salzburg.

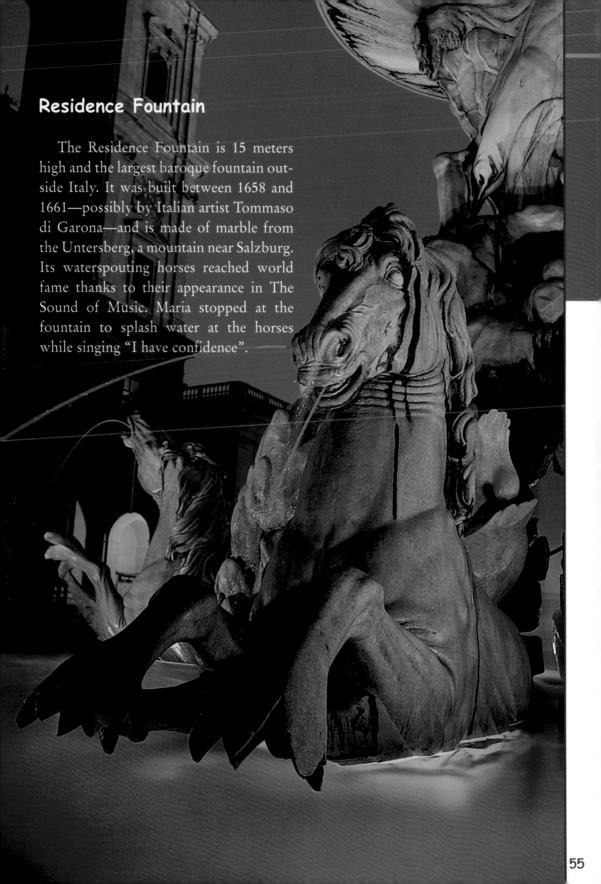

Residence Fountain

The Residence Fountain is 15 meters high and the largest baroque fountain outside Italy. It was built between 1658 and 1661—possibly by Italian artist Tommaso di Garona—and is made of marble from the Untersberg, a mountain near Salzburg. Its waterspouting horses reached world fame thanks to their appearance in The Sound of Music. Maria stopped at the fountain to splash water at the horses while singing "I have confidence".

Picture to the right: St. Peter's Cemetery and Church at dusk.

Picture below: The peaceful area of St. Peter's Abbey is the right place to recover from the sometimes hectic old town of Salzburg.

St. Peter's District

St. Peter's District really is the oldest part of Salzburg. The first monks, headed by Saint Rupert, settled here. The rest of the city started to spread out slowly around the monastery. Today you can still see catacombs cut in the rock of the Mönchsberg and originating from 215 A.D. St. Peter's cemetery is the oldest one in Austria still in use. Only priests and monks were buried here up to the year 1454. The arcades around the cemetery are family vaults from the 17th century with various examples of wrought iron work.

Obviously, St. Peter's Cemetery was a good inspiration for the movie makers: It was rebuilt in the hollywood studios for the scene when the Nazis were searching for the von Trapps and the family was hiding behind the tombstones. St. Peter's Church can also be seen in the opening scene.

Frohnburg Castle

The baroque Frohnburg Castle was built in the 17th century as a country house for the prince archbishops. Its façade, courtyard and front gate were used for the Trapp Villa in the film. Maria arrived here, after dancing along the Hellbrunn Alley, to meet the von Trapps for the first time. The baron tore the flag down from above the castle's doorway when they returned from their honeymoon and heard about the German occupation of Austria. They pushed their car noiselessly out of the castle's gate when they tried to escape. Today, the castle houses music students from the Mozarteum Music Academy.

Hellbrunn Palace

Hellbrunn Palace—just a few kilometers south of the city—was built between 1613 and 1619 under the orders of Markus Sittikus von Hohenems. As the archbishop had spent part of his life in Italy he tried to recreate an Italian atmosphere in this castle and its gardens. Unlike many other palaces, Hellbrunn has undergone no style changes and so, even today, the visitor can enjoy the lively southern scenery of this renaissance park.

Pictures to the right (from above): the Hellbrunn "Big-Mouth" moves its eyes and sticks out its tongue only with the use of water power; the "Monatsschlössl"; the fountains of the Hellbrunn Roman Theater; the illusionistic secco painting in the 90 square meter Grand Hall of the palace.
Picture below: Hellbrunn Palace, built by Italian architect Santino Solari.

The Gazebo at Hellbrunn

One of the main sites from the film is the glass gazebo, setting for various love scenes, like "Sixteen Going on Seventeen" and "Something Good". After a complete renovation, it was reconstructed in the park of Hellbrunn Palace. This is not the original setting, which was the garden of Leopoldskron Castle, but a more accessible one for visitors.

Pictures below: the park (left) and the Archbishop's Table at the trick fountains.

The artificial water games in Hellbrunn with numerous grottoes, trick fountains and the mechanical toy theater were built to entertain the noble guests of Archbishop Markus Sittikus. The impressive frescoes in the palace halls are masterpieces of the 17th century by Donato Mascagni from Florence.

Leopoldskron Castle

Leopoldskron Castle is the most beautiful rococo building in the Salzburg region. It was built in 1731 by Archbishop Leopold Count Firmian as a residence for his family. After 1837—when the Firmian family sold the estate—the building changed owners many times. Leopoldskron was a gallery, then became property of a landlord, and even the King of Bavaria can be found under the list of owners.

When famous writer Max Reinhardt, founder of the Salzburg Festival, bought it in 1918, it was in sad condition. Reinhardt renovated it, however, to its original beauty and used its garden for theater performances. Since 1958, Leopoldskron Castle has been owned by the "Salzburg Seminar in American Studies", an institution that focuses on economy problems.

Leopoldskron Castle was one of the most important locations for the film: The rear view was used for the Trapp family home. The family drank lemonade with the baroness on the terrace. Maria and the baron danced on the balcony during the ball scene, and the children fell into the adjacent lake. The Venetian room from the castle was copied and used as the ballroom for the interior shootings which were done in the studios.

Castle Anif of neogothic style was built in the 19th century as a summer residence for the Bishops of Chiemsee, Bavaria. Today, it is the property of the Count Moy family. It is of historical interest because the last Bavarian King, Ludwig II, abdicated here in 1918. The castle can be spotted in the beginning of the film, during the aerial view of the Salzburg region.

Untersberg

The Untersberg—a peak jutting 1,853 meters out of the Salzburg basin—offers a great view across the region. Climbing it takes more then two hours and should not be attempted without proper footware and windbreaker, as well as food and water provisions. Because there are some steep parts, you should not be afraid of heights.

You can reach the station of the cable car by catching bus No. 55 from the city center. The return trip, up and down, costs less then twenty US-dollars.

The Untersberg can be spotted twice in the movie: In the opening scene and in the escape scene, when the family climbs the mountain to leave the country.

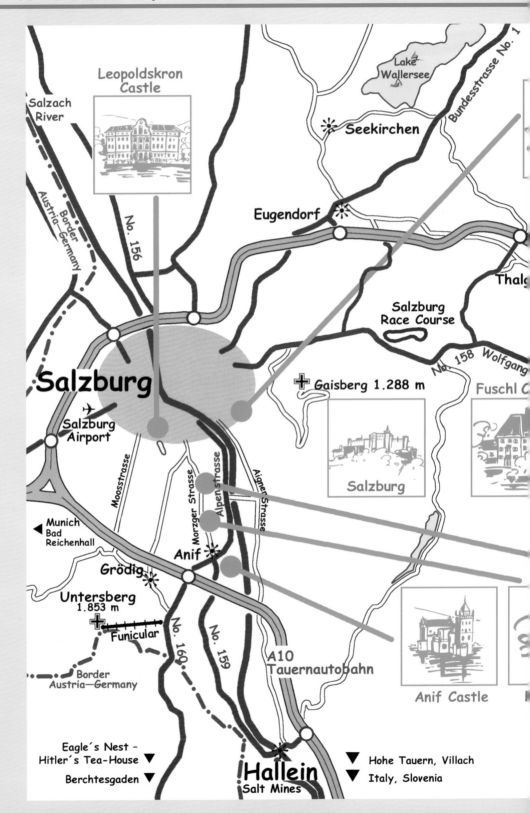

Leopoldskron Castle

Salzach River

Lake Wallersee

Seekirchen

Bundesstrasse No. 1

Border Austria—Germany

No. 156

Eugendorf

Thalg

Salzburg Race Course

Salzburg

Salzburg

Salzburg Airport

Gaisberg 1.288 m

No. 158 Wolfgang

Fuschl C

Moosstrasse

Morzger Strasse

Alpenstrasse

Aigner Strasse

Salzburg

◄ Munich Bad Reichenhall

Anif

Grödig

Untersberg 1.853 m

Funicular

No. 160

No. 159

A10 Tauernautobahn

Anif Castle

Border Austria—Germany

Eagle's Nest – Hitler's Tea-House ▼

Berchtesgaden ▼

Hallein Salt Mines

▼ Hohe Tauern, Villach
▼ Italy, Slovenia

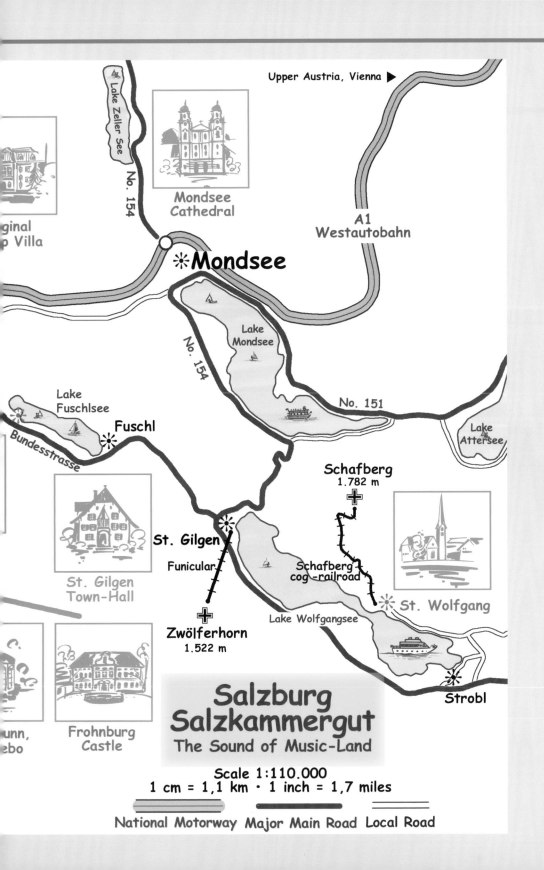

Upper Austria, Vienna ▶

Lake Zeller See

No. 154

Mondsee
Cathedral

A1
Westautobahn

ginal
p Villa

☀ **Mondsee**

No. 154

Lake
Mondsee

No. 151

Lake
Attersee

Lake
Fuschlsee

Bundesstrasse

☀ **Fuschl**

Schafberg
1.782 m

☀ St. Gilgen

Funicular

Schafberg
cog-railroad

☀ St. Wolfgang

St. Gilgen
Town-Hall

Zwölferhorn
1.522 m

Lake Wolfgangsee

☀ Strobl

unn,
ebo

Frohnburg
Castle

Salzburg
Salzkammergut
The Sound of Music-Land

Scale 1:110.000
1 cm = 1,1 km · 1 inch = 1,7 miles

National Motorway Major Main Road Local Road

Hohenwerfen Fortress

A motorway leads to the little village of Werfen which lies about 40 kilometers south from downtown Salzburg. The fortress was built under the rule of Archbishop Gebhardt von Helffenstein in the year 1077 to protect and defend the pass leading into the Salzburg basin.

Werfen is also the gateway for a trip to the famous Giant Ice Caves. A guide takes you into the spectacular cave system which is said to be biggest in the world.

Picture below: The Hohenwerfen Fortress gives Julie Andrews and the children a perfect background for "Do-Re-Mi".

The "Salzkammergut" Lake District

Generally speaking, the "Salzkammergut" extends over the entire area of lakes belonging to the Alps and Lower Alps. Three Austrian provinces—Salzburg, Styria, and Upper Austria—share this unique countryside. The Salzburg part is not only an area of great beauty but was also a welcome scenery for the Sound of

Picture: A prominent peak of the Salzkammergut—the Schafberg—is accessible to

Fuschl Castle and the village of St. Gilgen

The Fuschlsee is the first lake you reach when you enter the Salzkammergut from Salzburg. It is said to be the clearest and cleanest of the Salzkammergut lakes and offers great and untouched beaches.

Before you reach the village of Fuschl —a popular summer resort—you pass the Fuschl Castle. It was built as a hunting palace for the archbishops of Salzburg in the 15th century and is a first-class hotel today. It was seen in an aerial view at the beginning of The Sound of Music.

St. Gilgen is situated on another popular lake of the Salzkammergut, the Wolfgangsee. Mozart's mother, Anna Pertl, was born here. That is why a little Mozart museum has been set up in the city center.

Top: Lake Wolfgangsee and St. Gilgen
Middle: Hunting Palace at Fuschl
Bottom: Village of St. Wolfgang with its famous lakeside inn "Zum Weißen Rößl"

Village of St. Wolfgang Town and Lake Mondsee

St. Wolfgang is also situated on Wolfgangsee. Maybe the village is the most beautiful spot in the region, however, for sure it's the most touristy one, especially the lakeside inn "Zum Weißen Rössl".

A large cathedral dominates the small town of Mondsee. It was once the heart of an important monastery. Founded in 748 on the ruins of a roman settlement, it influenced the culture of the region for more than a thousand years until it was dissolved in 1792. The wedding scene in the movie was filmed here. Maria, led by Liesl, walked down the aisle to meet the baron in front of the stairs of the main altar.

Top: The large cathedral of Mondsee village; Middle: Inside the church—here, the wedding scenes were shot; Bottom left: Lakes Mondsee, Attersee; Bottom right: The Schafberg cog railway can also be spotted in the motion picture.

The "Original Sound Of Music Tour"
arranged by Panorama Tour is something
nobody should miss.

You see not only the places used in
the film "Sound Of Music" but you are
also taken through the most beautiful
part of the land of Salzburg, the "Salzkammergut" with its lakes and mountains, villages with century old churches
and houses profusely decorated with flowers
on their balconies.

You hear friendly and witty expla-
nations of places and their history as well
as of the life of the Trapp Family in several
different languages while you lean back
on very comfortable seats and let the most
beautiful scenery pass by.

There are stops on the way where you
can stretch your legs, go shopping, re-appear
in Austrian outfit – or get a taste of the finest
Austrian "Kirch & Torten" or with coffee or have
the best "Würstel with mustard" you can
dream of.

Don't miss it – I never do !!!

Maria von Trapp

The Sound of Music-Tour

The Sound of Music Tour was born when first visitors came to Salzburg in 1965, shortly after the release of the film, trying to find locations like the lakeside castle or the gazebo. The Panorama drivers had been involved with the filming of The Sound of Music for months, so they were able to arrange a sightseeing tour. They also knew a lot of gossip about the filming, so the tour soon became popular.

Over the last couple of years it has matured to an extensive Salzburg city and lake district tour which not only takes its guests to the settings of the movie but also leads to the main cultural attractions of the region. To see the Salzkammergut lake district is a "must" for every visitor, so take the tour to not miss out!

Top left: Maria von Trapp has been on the Sound of Music Tour many times and left tour operator "Panorama" with a letter of recommendation.

Bottom photos: Famous guests on the tour: Maria von Trapp (with tour guide Craig Mitchell) and Christopher Plummer (left with "Panorama" operator Stefan Herzl). Panorama Tours can also be found on the Internet: www.panoramatours.at